ADVENTURES with ZAP

107 Creative Prompts FOR Beginning Writers

DIANE LANDY

Illustrated by

ALLISON HERSHEY

THE EXPERIMENT

NEW YORK

ADVENTURES WITH ZAP: *107 Creative Prompts for Beginning Writers*
Copyright © 2018 by Diane Landy
Illustrations copyright © 2018 by Allison Hershey

The Experiment, LLC
220 East 23rd Street, Suite 600
New York, NY 10010-4658
theexperimentpublishing.com

The Experiment's books are available at special discounts when purchased in bulk for premiums and sales promotions as well as for fund-raising or educational use. For details, contact us at info@theexperimentpublishing.com.

Library of Congress Cataloging-in-Publication Data

Names: Landy, Diane, author. | Hershey, Allison, illustrator.
Title: Adventures with Zap : 107 creative prompts for beginning writers /
Diane Landy ; illustrated by Allison Hershey.
Description: New York : The Experiment, [2018] | Audience: Age 4 to 8.
Identifiers: LCCN 2017060925 | ISBN 9781615194414 (pbk.)
Subjects: LCSH: English language--Composition and exercises--Study and
teaching (Elementary)--Juvenile literature. | Creative writing (Elementary
education)--Juvenile literature. | Prompting (Education)--Juvenile
literature.
Classification: LCC LB1576 .L268 2018 | DDC 372.62/3--dc23 LC record available at https://lccn.loc.gov/2017060925

ISBN 978-1-61519-441-4

Cover and text design by Sarah Smith

Manufactured in China
Distributed by Workman Publishing Company, Inc.
Distributed simultaneously in Canada by the University of Toronto Press

First printing June 2018
10 9 8 7 6 5 4 3 2 1

To Brian, Sarah, Jenna, Cristobal, & James.

—D. L.

To W. A. Gibson (Grampa), whose drawings made grammar fun.

—A. F. H.

How This Book Was Born

Hi! I'm Zap. When I flew to your blue planet, I met an Earthling named Libery Ann. Her house was FULL of books. She let me borrow one to take home to Vox Nova.

Zots! Strange creatures lived inside that book. I wanted to know their stories but I didn't know how to read. Words looked like weird squiggles lined up in rows.

So guess what I did? I made up stories from the pictures. Once I got home, a friend wrote them down.

One day—*zzzzzap!*—I got an idea. What if Earth kids had a special book they could write in, too? Then we could share!

When I get a good idea, I catch it and hold tight. Then I play with my idea and ask someone to help me write. A little bit every day. THAT's how books are born.

Now you are holding the book I made for you. Comics inside tell my story. I added lots of ideas for tales you can tell and art you can draw. That means YOU become an author and illustrator of OUR book! For reals!!!

Ready? Set? GO! Let's play with words and pictures.

Your pencil pal from outer space,

Zap

You were born on planet Earth.

This is me in my spaceship.

I was born on Vox Nova.

Create YOUR title page for OUR book.

_____ 's

Add your first name to the title!

Adventures with Zap

Written and
illustrated by _____

Your first and last names go here

I dedicate this book to _____

Note a special person or helper here

The day I started to
write with Zap _____

Month, day, and year go here

Paste a photo or draw a picture of yourself here:

How to Use This Book

It's simple. Just turn on your brain. Then fill the blank spaces with drawings and words. Need ideas? You got it. There are plenty of prompts marked with a  Or use ideas of your own. YOU choose what to say, either true or make-believe.

Need writing lines? Add them. Want to write sideways? Or draw upside down? Go for it. This is a place to **Play!**

Can't Write Yet?

That's OK. Neither can I. But we'll learn how to soon. Until then, you can use my magic spell! First you have to hunt for a helper who has time, like Uncle Fergus or your sitter. (I chose my best friend, Gooey,) Then wave your magic pencil wand and say, "Zip-zapper-zot. You're my robot!" *Ka-Bloing!* That person becomes your reading, writing robot. A robot that writes EXACTLY what you say. (Don't worry. The robot spell won't last forever.)

Learning to Write?

My friend Gooey is, too! She promised to teach me. Once you know your letter sounds, you can start to write. Want to know her secret?

S-l-o-w-l-y say the word you want to write. Then write each letter you hear. If you hear a mysterious sound, put a blank in its place. Earthlings call this "invented spelling." Zots! You're an inventor!

I namd MI kat fr_skee

Prefer correct spelling? Go to adventureswithzap.com for info.

Already a Writer?

Lucky word wizard. I wish I were you! Did you know authors do rewrites to make good writing great? For reals! Want to be a great writer? Try CRAMS:

CROSS OUT parts that repeat or make you fall asleep.

READ your story aloud. If anything sounds goofy, fix it.

ADD cool details, like these:

Sounds

Crack!

Talking

"Look! A mermaid!"

Smells
The cheese smelled like dirty soccer socks.

MOVE anything that's out of order or your reader will go bonkers.

SWAP blah words with lively words that paint a picture in your head:

The boy ~~was small~~ stood in my hand.

Changes are called edits. Double zots! You can be an editor!

Tips for Parents and Helpers

Need help to get going? Oral storytelling is a natural way to start.

Find a comfy spot and read the comics together. Then read the first comic prompt on page 6. When your child has finished drawing, say, "Tell me about your spaceship and I'll write what you say." Then write what is said, word for word. Try to dig deeper: "How does that gizmo work?" and "What foods will you pack?" A great way to wrap up is to read your child's words out loud and give the gift of encouragement.

Above all, inspire a love of writing with a playful experience. Keep sessions short at first and let go of mistakes. Try to create a routine that works for your family. Fifteen minutes at bedtime? While waiting for a sibling? Over summer break?

For more tips, check out adventureswithzap.com.

About Me

 Introduce yourself to Zap. Finish writing the sentences below.

Hi, my name is ___diYa___ . I am ___7___ years old.

The best thing about being my age is . . .

The worst thing about being my age is . . .

A secret about me no one else knows is . . .

Pssst...
I'm scared of
green ants.

What are some of your favorite things on Earth?

My favorite game

My favorite shoes

My favorite sound

My favorite _____

You choose

 Draw a picture of your family.

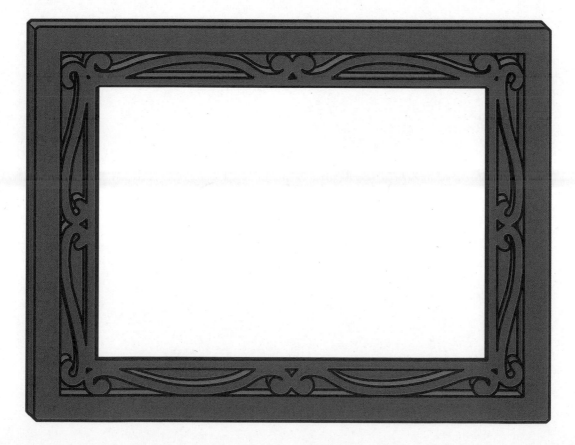

 Pretend you have a spaceship. Draw a picture of it here.

The spaceship crashed on earth. It came from the moon. There were 10 aliens in the spaceship that crashed. The spaceship fell apart when it crashed and the aliens tried to fix it.

They couldn't fix it. So they called the alien garage. And it got fixed.

 Prepare to test your pilot skills on a spaceship adventure. What will you pack? What will you take to remind you of home? Make a list.

 Count down and lift off. Imagine flying your spaceship over the place where you live. Draw what you see.

Write about your flight. How do you control your spaceship?
What does it feel like to fly?

 Where on Earth would you like to go? Pretend to land your spaceship there. Draw a picture of this place.

Play a guessing game. Write clues about the place where you landed. Read your clues aloud and have someone guess where you are.

CLUE **1** The weather here is . . .

CLUE **2** When I look around, I see . . .

CLUE **3** When I listen, I hear . . .

 What is the strangest creature you have ever seen on Earth, on land or in the water? Draw a picture for Zap. Label your picture with the name of this animal.

Write a note to tell Zap about the creature in your picture.
Share what it looks like. Describe where it lives.

Hi, Zap,

Your friend, _____

 Invent a wacky way to travel, like a trampoline train, a roller-coaster kayak, or an itty-bitty bubble bus. Play with ideas. Draw a picture of yourself on the go.

Write about your drawing. What do you call this wacky way to travel? Use fun words and silly sounds to describe how you are moving.

Zurrrg!

I'm stuck! What on
Earth do I write?

When you wonder what to write . . .

BRAINSTORM!

A brainstorm is a speedy burst of ideas.

Big ideas. Little ideas. Silly, good, and bad ideas. All ideas count! You can brainstorm by yourself or in a group. It's a great way to solve problems, too, like how to get your sister to let you into her cosmic fort.

Brainstorming is as easy as 1-2-3!

1. Ask any question.

2. In a minute or more, write every idea that pops into your head. The more ideas the better. Wild ideas welcome!

 Pop-ity Pop POP!

3. Choose your favorite idea and write,

write,

write!

ZAP'S SAMPLE
(with help from a friend):

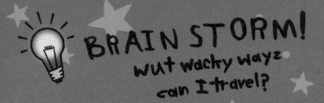

BRAIN STORM!
Wut wacky wayz
can I travel?

shoot_ng star

water
slide
sity

lazer
skees

Fish
peeple
see
sled

sand
doon
sale bote

purpol
pikel
barrel

Piggybak
on a
Wale!

on the
sholder
of a jient
fromper
stomp

roket
sox

Pssst . . .
I circled my best
idea!

Try it!

BRAINSTORM!

What wacky ways
can I travel?

 Where do you wish to sleep? On a bunk bed? In a castle? At a campout on Saturn? Or . . . ? Draw a picture.

Pretend to get comfy in the place you wish to sleep. What do you hear? Share what you like about sleeping in this spot. Make a wish upon a star.

 Your test flight was a success! It's time to circle the moon and fly home. What's the first thing you do when you land? Draw a picture.

Pretend to call Zap on the phone. *Rrr–ring!* "Hello?" Tell him something exciting about your flight or share some news. Write what you and Zap say.

Me:

Zap:

Me:

Zap:

Me:

 Zeeks! Zap is scared. On Zap's faces below, draw his mouth, eyes, and antennae to show different feelings. Add eyebrows and eyelids if you want.

Happy

Sad

Mad

Grrr-umpy

Surprised

Grossed out

Choose one feeling and write about it. What makes you feel this way? What do you say? What do you do?

I feel _____ when . . .

Write the feeling you chose

 Draw a picture of a time you fell down and got hurt.

Close your eyes and remember your fall like it's a movie in your mind. Then write about it. What were you doing? What made you fall? Describe your pain.

 Invent your own robot. Think what size and shape you want it to be. Draw a picture. Title your art with a name for your robot.

_____

Title

Write about your robot. How did you build it? What sounds does it make? What can your robot do?

Don't forget to brainstorm if you get stuck.

 Think of a time that you were surprised. Draw a picture of what happened.

Write about your picture. Who (or what) surprised you and how? What did you say? What did you like or not like about being surprised?

 Pretend you have a superpower. Do you wear a costume? Draw a picture of yourself using your power. Title your art with your superhero name.

Title

Stand up and use your power. Then sit down and write. What is your power? How do you make it work? What happens after you use it? Add a noise!

Want to Rocket-Boost Your Writing?

Use POWER Words!

 POWER words add zing, flair, and pop. They make your story come alive for your reader. Use them to launch your writing into the stratosphere. Look at Zap's examples. Then fill in the blanks with POWER words of your own!

ACTION

Action words show your reader what you or your character is DOING.

INSTEAD OF ...	Use a POWER word to SHOW detail:
FALL	Stumble, tumble, slip, _____
FLY	Zoom, glide, hover, _____
GO	Tiptoe, skip, slither, _____
PLAY	Bounce, race, flip, _____
SAY	Shout, moan, whisper, _____

SENSES

Sensory words let your reader SEE, HEAR, SMELL, TASTE, and TOUCH.

When you want to . . .	Use a POWER word to SHOW detail:
SEE	Pea-size, sparkly, rusty, _____
HEAR	Crunch, BANG, splat, _____
SMELL	Moldy, sour, clean, _____
TASTE	Chocolaty, burned, spicy, _____
TOUCH	Thorny, fluffy, cold as steel, _____

TRAITS

Trait words help your reader know the CHARACTERS in your story.

When your character is . . .	Use a POWER word to SHOW detail:
BAD	Wicked, bossy, greedy, _____
GOOD	Heroic, honest, helpful, _____
FUN	Curious, silly, adventurous, _____

 If you could be any animal on Earth, what animal would you be?
Draw a picture. Label your picture with the name of this animal.

Get up and move like your animal. Pretend to find food. Then sit down to write. What POWER words SHOW how you moved? Write as many as you can think of.

What do you like most about being this animal?

 Pretend you find a pet from another planet. Draw a picture. Title your art with a name for your pet.

_____

Title

Write about your space alien pet. It's as big or as small as a . . . what? When you pat it on the back, what does it feel like? How do you play with this pet?

Your pet will come ALIVE when you use POWER words. For reals!

Imagine you are the chef of a restaurant on Vox Nova. What unusual foods might you create? Draw a drink, main course, and dessert to make a menu.

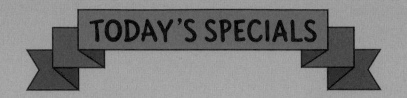

TODAY'S SPECIALS

Main Course

Drink

Dessert

Are you hungry? Do you want some sticky stars with bubble dip?

Name each item on your menu and describe how it tastes.

_____

Name of your drink

_____

Name of your main course

_____

Name of your dessert

 Pretend to wake up in the morning. *Yawn!* When you get out of bed, you say, "Ka-zooks! What's this? I have a tail!" Draw a picture of yourself.

Write about your tail. Share what it looks like and feels like to touch. How do you use your new tail? What would you say if someone pulled it?

 Think of a time you were frightened. Draw a picture of what startled you.

Write about your picture. Where were you? What happened? Show details like movements and sounds. How did you react?

 Draw a picture of a time your feelings were hurt.

Write about your picture. Share how your feelings got hurt. What did you say or do? What happened next?

🔆 BRAINSTORM!

What could I name the critter Meow sees?

Begin to write a story about the critter from Vox Nova. Title your story
with a name from your brainstorm. Describe where it lives. What does
it want?

_____

Title

Pretend you are the critter. Write your thoughts inside the bubble.

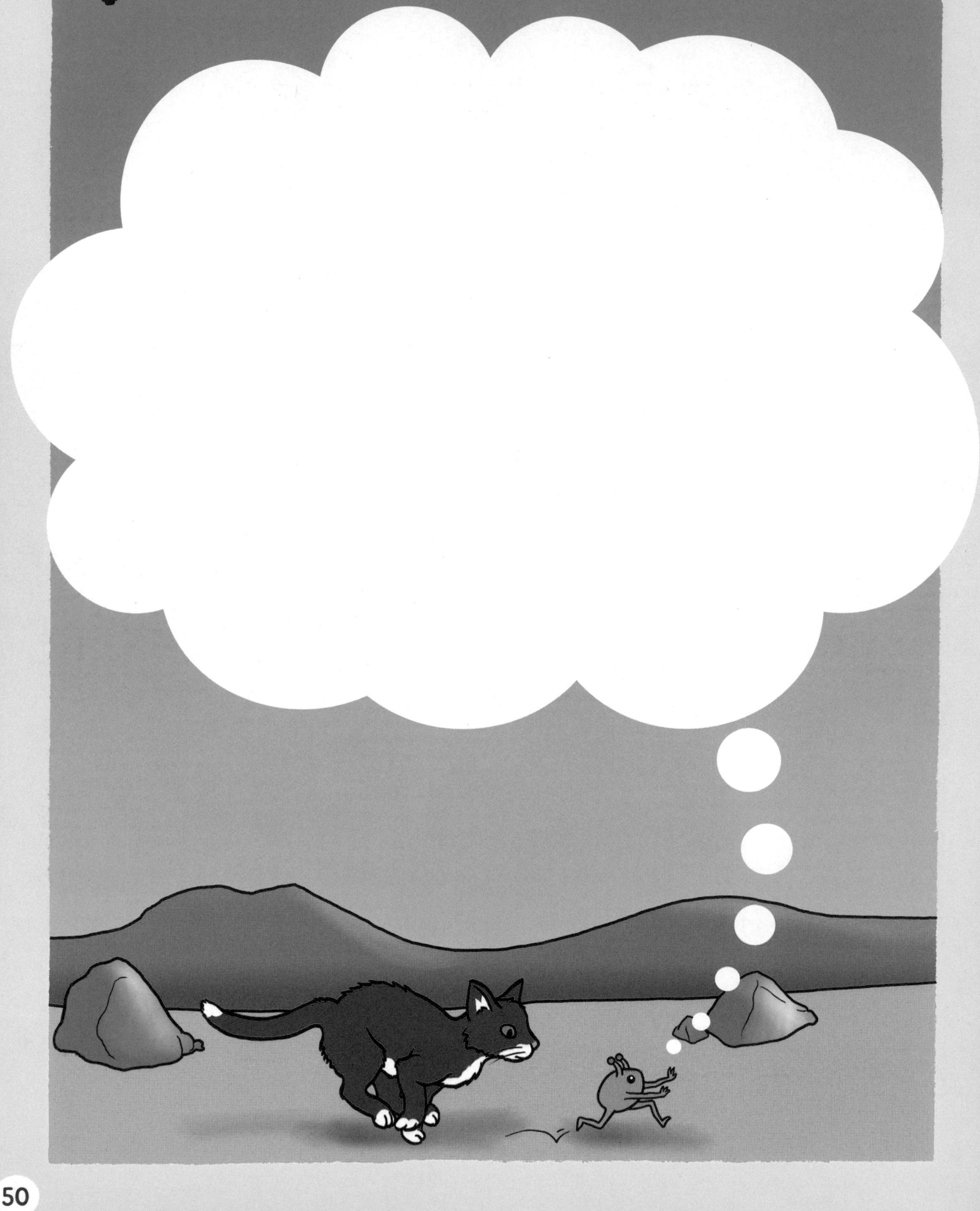

Pretend you are Zap. Write your thoughts inside the bubble.

Where is your favorite place to hide? Under, behind, or inside . . . what? Draw a picture. Label your picture with the place you are hiding.

Write about your hideout. What makes you hide? How do you fit into your spot? How do you feel when you are hiding?

 Where would you like to build a playhouse? Behind the sofa? In a tree? Up, up, UP on the moon or under the sea? Or . . . ? Draw a picture.

Invite Zap into your playhouse. What is the first thing you show him?
Write about how it works or what makes it special.

 Pretend you see a scary monster on another planet. Draw a picture. Title your picture with a spook-tacular name for your monster.

_____
Title

Write about your scary monster. How does it move? What does it want? How do you tame it?

Use POWER words to show how you tame your sc-c-c-ary monster!

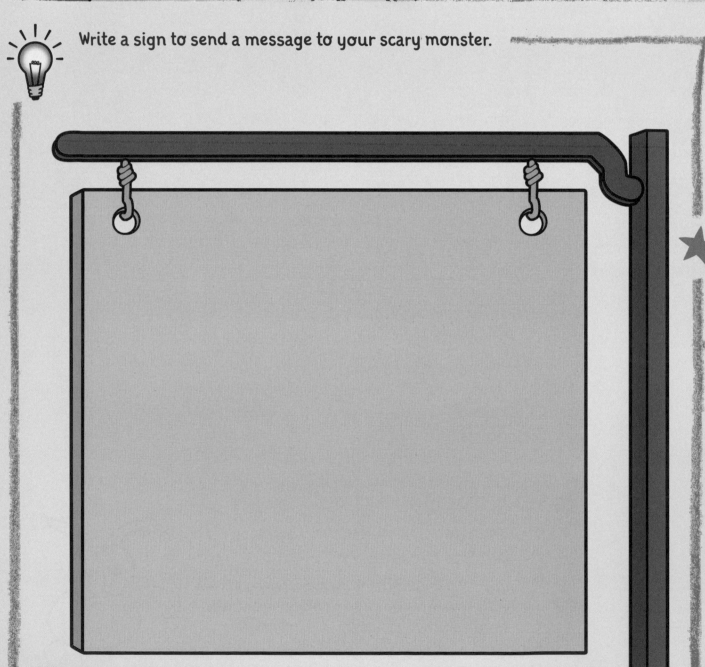

Write a sign to send a message to your scary monster.

If you had a sign, what would it say? A welcome message? A riddle? A rule for visitors? Or . . . ? Write it down!
(Want more sign designs? Go to adventureswithzap.com.)

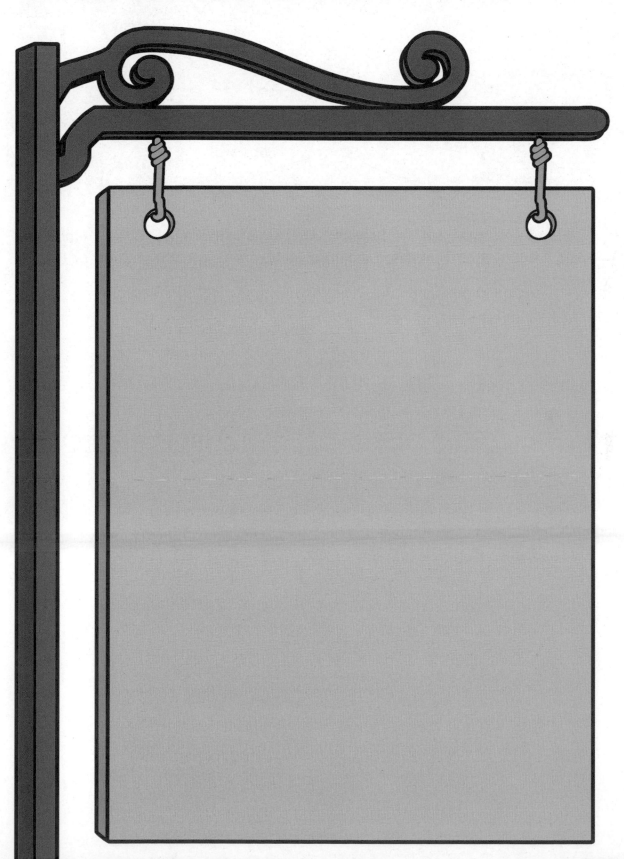

 Pretend you meet a friendly monster from another planet. Draw a picture. Add a noise that it makes. Title your picture with a kooky name for your monster.

_____

Title

Write about your friendly monster. How does it move? What does it want? How do you help it get what it wants?

What is Meow thinking? Write Meow's thoughts inside the bubble.

What is Zap thinking? Write Zap's thoughts inside the bubble.

 Draw a comic of two space alien friends having a disagreement. Add dialogue bubbles if you want.

Pssst . . . *Dialogue* is a writer's word for talking.

Write what it's like to argue with a friend. What can friends do to be agreeable again?

Zots! Let's write a letter to Libery Ann. She'll know what to do.

65

Hey, word wizards. Try to correct Gooey's letter. Not a word wizard yet? Read the letter and skip to the next page.

Let's start with, "Hi Libery Ann..."

Hi Libery Ann,

It's Zap. ~~Remimbr~~ Remember me? Ges Wut?

A bad thing hapnd. ~~Win~~ When I wuz n yor

howze, a monstr namd Meeow snuk

insid mi spayship! Aftr I landid it

atakd me and a criter. Now its is

~~tuz loos~~ on Yor nova!!! I haf to stop it

befor it hurts sum wan els.

Help!!!!!!   Wut shud I do?

Heer is a pikcher.

PS. Gooey sez sheez

Sory for the spel_ng mistaks.

i sed its ok wen yor lern_ng.

yor frend,
Zap

Zoops! Zap needs your help. Fix the labels on his drawing.

BRAINSTORM!

What dangerous animals live on planet Earth?

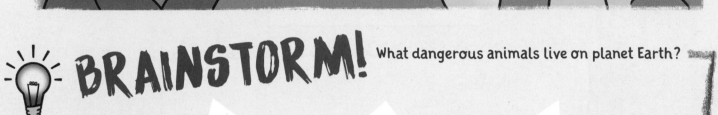

Oh, no! Pretend an animal in your brainstorm is loose in your town! You are a TV news anchor. Draw your face on the TV. Write what you say to warn Earthlings.

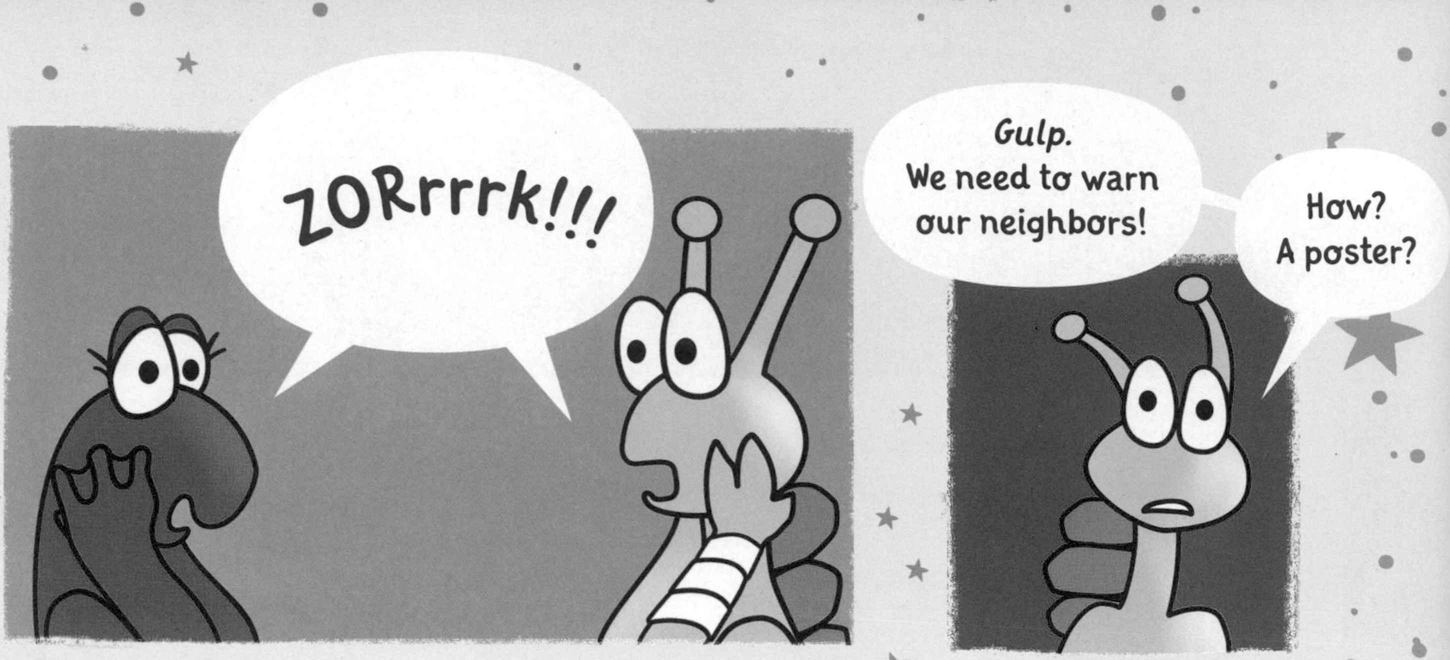
ZORrrrk!!!
Gulp. We need to warn our neighbors!
How? A poster?

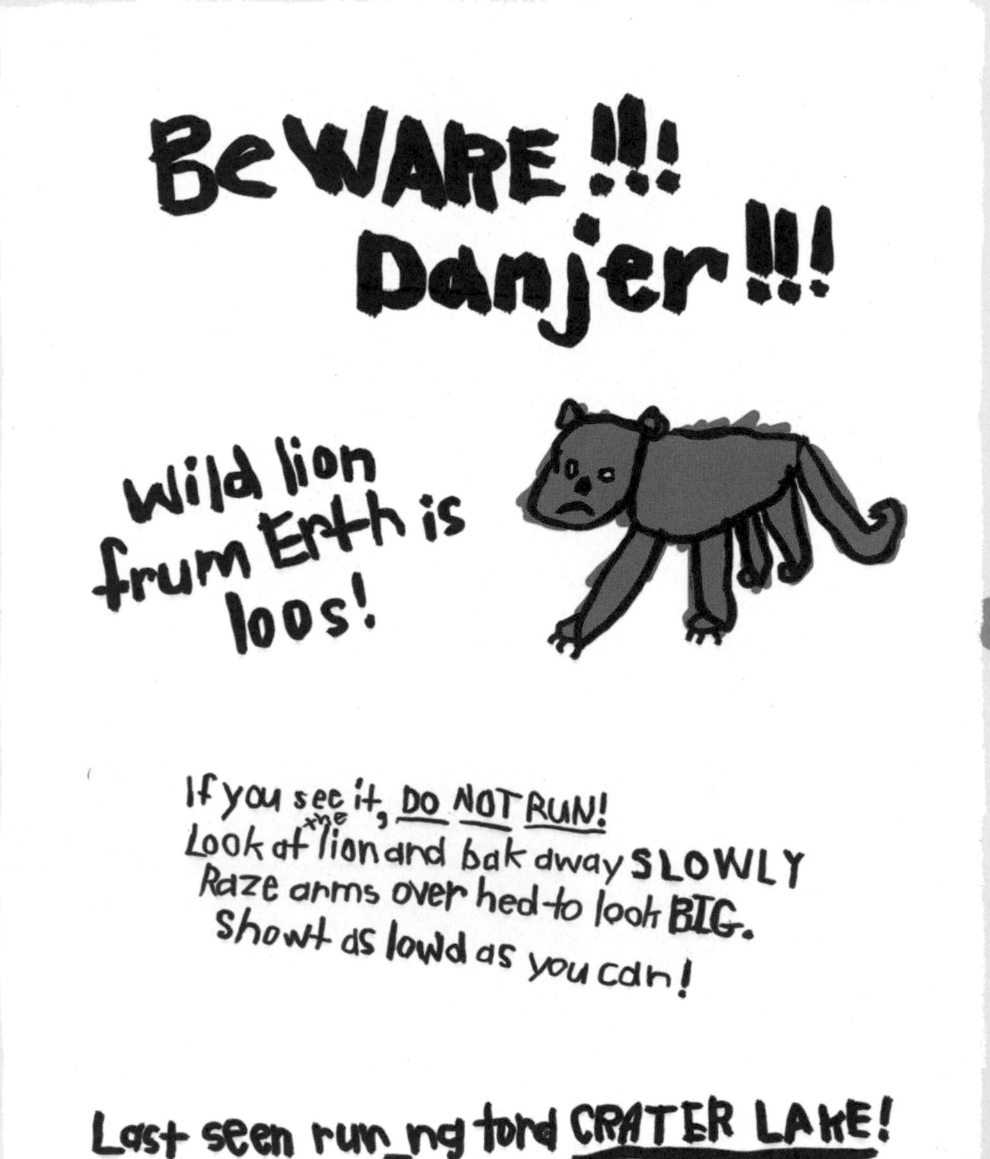
BeWARE !!!
Danjer !!!
Wild lion frum Erth is loos!
If you see it, DO NOT RUN!
Look at the lion and bak away SLOWLY
Raze arms over hed to look BIG.
Showt as lowd as you can!
Last seen run_ng tord CRATER LAKE!

Make a poster for yourself. Need to warn your neighbors?
Have something to give or sell? Want to run for president? Or . . . ?
Write and draw what you want.

Who would love to get a letter from you? Grandpop? The Tooth Fairy? The messy leprechaun in your attic? Or . . . ? Make a list of names.

72

CAT CARE GUIDE

Dear Zap,

I'll never forget the day you landed at our little library. After you left, families gathered here to share tales of a UFO. Most grown-ups thought your spaceship was a fancy, new drone. I should have snapped a photo to prove you were here!

The animal in your drawing is a cat. It's probably someone's precious pet. Do not be frightened, Zap. Cats are usually harmless if you are kind.

The cat needs to be cared for. Can you do it? If you can't, find a Vox Novan who can. Enclosed is a booklet that tells all you need to know about feeding, housing, and playing with a cat.

A pet is a big responsibility. Please write again to let me know how it goes.

Sincerely,

Luna Osman, Librarian (aka Libery Ann ☺)

P.S. Your library book is due. You must renew or return it.

P.P.S. Children asked if they could write to you. I said, "Absolutely!"

Hi Zap,

We put up flyers around the library with your picture of Meow.

Hope that helps!

Bye for now,

Jade and Kai

Howdy Zap,

Our cat Bandit is sneaky too! She sneaks inside our cubirds and londry basket. Bandit would sneak in your spaceship if you landed on our balkony. Want to see? We live in apartmint 3E. When can you come over?

Later gator,

Asher, August & Nate

Zap, listen to this one!

Zap,

Here is something you should know. Signs a cat will attack:

1. Makes a growling sound

2. Flattens ears

3. Arches back

If you see any of these signs, **BACK OFF!**

Sinsiraly,

Shamone

Hello Zap,
You are lucky. Your monster is only a kitty.
I wish I had a kitty monster.
Mom is a lergie so she said no way.

Love, Leila

Dude,
Cats can't talk. Meow is a sound they make when they are hungry. Your cat needs a real name. How about Waffles?

Rats! Now I'm hungry for waffles. Meow!

See ya., DJ

DOGS RULE !!!

Hey Zap,

Meow might be homesick. Or scared of YOU! When he comes back, be nice. OK?

Your friend,

Sydney

P.S. I think you should call him Red Ball Jets

Huh? Gooey, what does this say?

Cats are nice.

My cat likes to snuggal

Dear Zap,

You'd like my stripy cat, Ping. She can do flips. And when she curls in my lap, she sings a purring song. Can you make Meow sing? Try petting behind her ears.

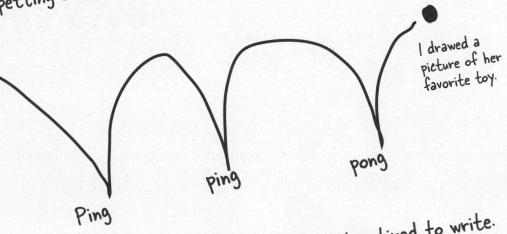

I drawed a picture of her favorite toy.

Ping

Ping

Pong

I have to go now. It's bedtime and Mom is too tired to write.

Your Bestest Friend Forever,

Alexandra Michelle Leesanderski

P.S. Wait! One more thing. Goodnight, Zap. Sweet dreams. Uh— oh. Mom's eyelids are clos

Hi Zap,

Meow is not a monstir. Cats are good. They cach mice in the kichen.

Yay! Then they eat them. Ick!

Your pen pal,
Izzy

Zapbud,

Come in. Do you copy? You should make a toy for Meow to chase. A leaf or feather tied to string is fun. My cat, General George, loves the one I made for him.

Earthbud out

Hola,

Don't be a scaredy cat! Ha ha ha haaa haaaaaaa. I hope you like my joke.

My uncle has a scratcher cat named Winston. I have to wear an oven mitt to pet him. Do they sell oven mitts on Vox Nova?

Adios Amigo,

Dakota

Zap, come on. We need to find Meow.

77

 What do you search for outside? Stardust? Bugs? Buried treasure? Or . . . ? Draw a collection of what you like to find. Label each thing. Circle your favorite.

Write a note to tell Zap about your favorite thing to find. Share how you find it. What does it feel like to hold? What makes it a keeper?

Zurrrg. I want to remind you of something, but I've forgotten what it is.

 Pretend you and your family have the noses of hound dogs. Draw a picture.

Zots! You smell things you never did before: brownies baking miles away (yum!) and a rotten tuna sandwich (yuck!). Write what you do with your fabulous sniffer.

 Think of a time you were bored while you waited. Where were you? Draw a picture.

Zots! While you are waiting, a robot suddenly shows up! What does it bring you? Use words to show what it is. What do you and the robot do next?

Now I remember! Don't forget to use TOWER words. Er . . . FLOWER words? No. POWER words!

 Pretend a five-eyed sloghopper snuck onto your spaceship. Invent a simple toy for it to play with. Draw a picture.

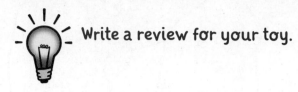 Write a review for your toy.

How does the sloghopper play with your toy? Use ACTION words!

How much do Earthlings pay for your toy? $ _____

Rate your toy using 1 to 5 stars:

1 STAR	2 STARS	3 STARS	4 STARS	5 STARS
No way!	Not good	So-so	A-OK	Best ever!

Color in the number of stars your toy deserves.

Easy to set up   ☆ ☆ ☆ ☆ ☆

Fun to play with   ☆ ☆ ☆ ☆ ☆

Makes the sloghopper move   ☆ ☆ ☆ ☆ ☆

Lasts a long time   ☆ ☆ ☆ ☆ ☆

Worth every penny   ☆ ☆ ☆ ☆ ☆

 Draw a picture of a time you were brave.

Write about your picture. What were you afraid might happen? How did you face your fear? Share what it felt like to be brave.

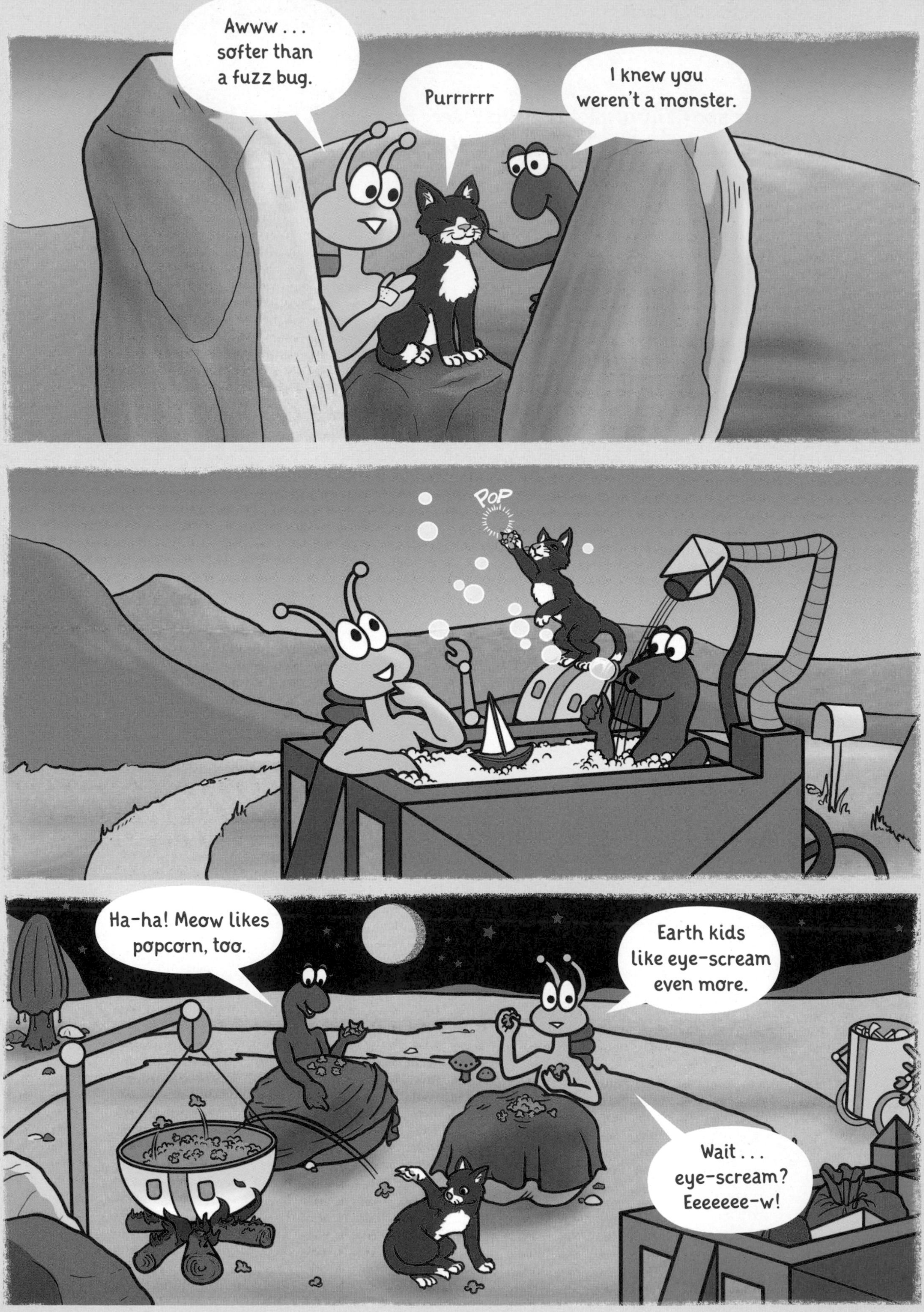
Awww . . . softer than a fuzz bug.
Purrrrrr
I knew you weren't a monster.
POP
Ha-ha! Meow likes popcorn, too.
Earth kids like eye-scream even more.
Wait . . . eye-scream? Eeeeeee-w!

What is a friend? Write what it means to you. Who is your best friend, either real or imagined? What do you love about this friend?

Dear Zap,

I thought my cat ran away. I've been calling her every day. "Sneakers! Here kitty, kitty!" My heart broke in pieces when she didn't come home.

Then today I saw a flyer outside the library that read, "Is your cat missing?"

"Yes, yes, YES!" I jumped up and clapped and ran home to tell Grandma. She didn't believe in you at first. Then I told her your drawing looked exactly like Sneakers when she's cranky.

"My stars," she said and had to sit for a minute.

Is it cold out in space? Sneakers might need a blanket since she's always on the lookout for a warm spot to nap. When she was just a kitten she slept in Dad's sneakers. He likes to leave them in the sun after every run. P-U!!! I bet your spaceship smells better than those shoes.

Please send my cat home. I really, really, REALLY miss my little Sneak-Sneak.

Your new friend from Earth,

Becca

P.S. I turn 10 in July. How old are you?

Meow's family has been found. Yay for Becca! Bummer for Zap. What if Zap keeps the cat? Becca will be upset. Write a note to convince Zap to change his mind.

 Think of a time you said goodbye when you did not want to. Draw a picture.

What is the hardest thing you have ever had to do? Write about it.

The hardest thing I ever had to do was . . .

I did not want to do this because . . .

After I did it I . . .

Invent space alien words for saying goodbye. Write Zap's and Gooey's words inside their dialogue bubbles.

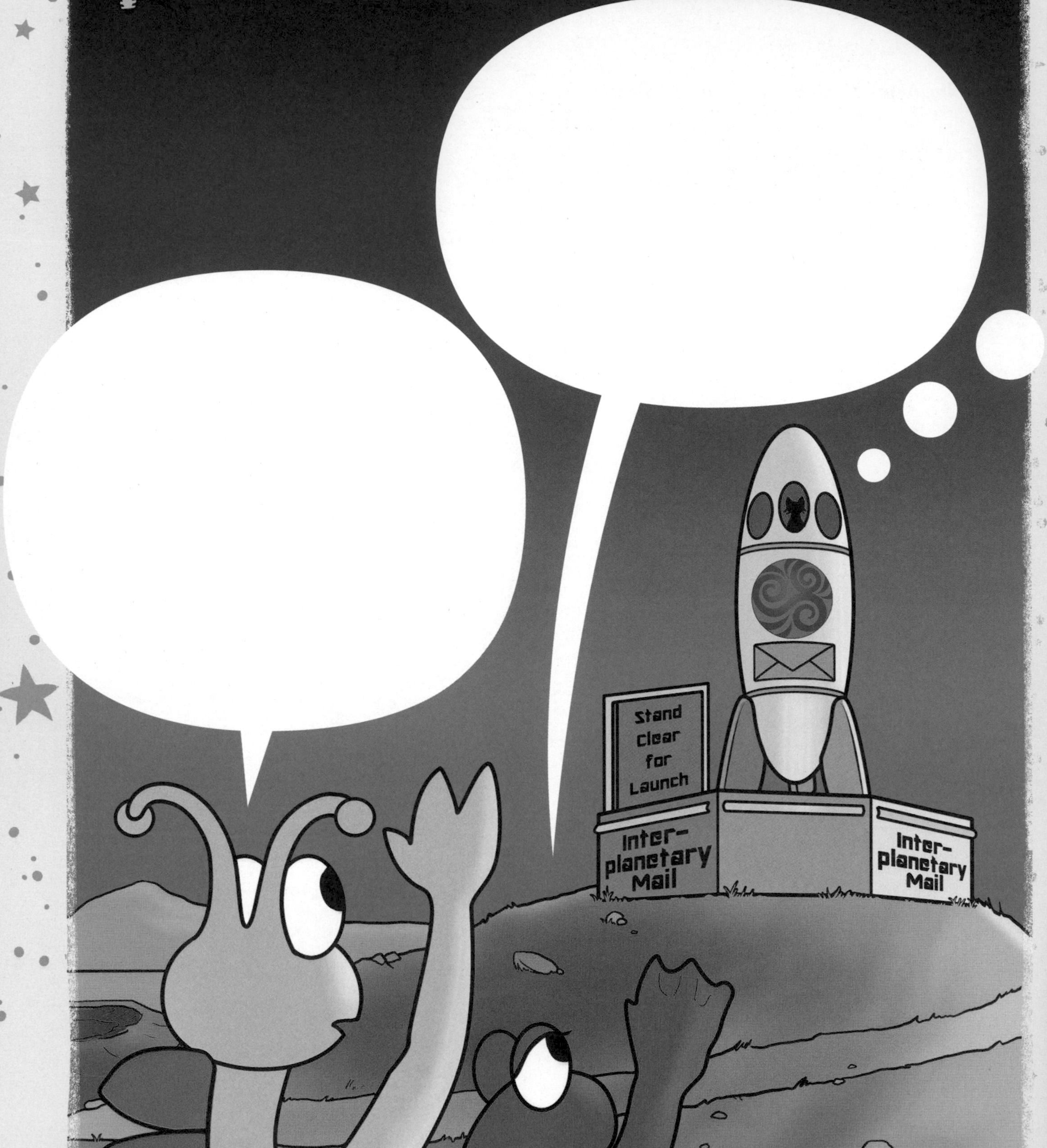

Stand Clear for Launch
Inter-planetary Mail
Inter-planetary Mail

Write what Sneakers is thinking inside the thought bubble.

TO ZAP

I promis
2 never
ever leev U

Yur Best Frend
4 ever
Gooey

When you do not feel well, how do other Earthlings help you feel better? How do you cheer yourself up? Write about the ways your mood can be lifted.

STEP 1

Draw a picture.

STEP 2

Use scissors to cut out the picture.

STEP 3

Tape the picture to a stick.

 What craft have you made that you are proud of? Or what craft would you like to make? A bookmark? A valentine? A decoration? Or . . . ? Draw a picture.

Write instructions so a friend can make your craft. What do you do first? Second? Third? Put each step in the order that you do it.

How to Make a

_____

Write the name of your craft

STEP **1**

STEP **2**

STEP **3**

 Where is your favorite place to play with other Earthlings? Draw a picture. Label your artwork with the name of this place.

Write about this place. Describe where you are and what you hear. How are you playing? What makes this your favorite place to play with other Earthlings?

Don't forget your POWER words to rocket-boost your writing! Need a review? Turn to pages 34 and 35.

 Pretend to send Zap a package with a gotta-have-it gadget or a tasty treat from Earth. Draw a picture of what you put inside the box.

What POWER words *show* what's in your box? Write as many as you can think of. Color? Weight? What is it made of? What does it feel like to touch or bite?

 Write Zap a short note to go with your package. Use one or more of your POWER words.

 What is the greatest present you were ever given? Draw a picture.

Write about your gift.

I was given a _____

What were you given?

From _____

Who gave you this present?

For _____

What was the occasion for getting this gift?

This present is amazing because . . .

I use it to . . .

ZOTS!
You just wrote
a thank-you
note!

105

Dear Zap,

A gazillion thanks for sending Sneakers home! I covered her in kisses and my heart is whole again.

We were on Channel 8 News! Now that Sneakers is famous, neighbors keep knocking on our door. They all want to meet my Outer Space Cat.

I saved the best part for last. Dad said you could come to my 10th birthday party! It's July 8 at 2 pm. Bring a towel for the beach.

Will you please fly back to Earth, Zap? I'll give you the best and biggest piece of cake!

Bear hugs and whisker tickles,

Becca and Sneakers

P.S. I hope you like your present. I picked it out myself.

Pretend you are turning 10 years old. It's time for a party!
Create an invitation for family and friends.

YOU ARE INVITED

TO A _____
Write the kind of party you are having (picnic, piñata, pumpkin carving, or . . . ?)

DATE _____   _____   _____
MONTH   DAY   YEAR

TIME _____ : _____ to _____ : _____
HOUR   MINUTES   HOUR   MINUTES

WHERE _____
Location or address

RSVP _____
Who should guests call to let you know if they can come?

PHONE (_____) _____ - _____

Write a short message for guests, such as what to bring
or something fun you will do:

_____

_____

_____

 Pretend to travel in a time machine to your future. *Za-whoosh!* Now you are 10 years old! What new skill do you have? Draw a picture.

Write about your picture. Use POWER words to show Zap your new talent. What do you like best about being 10? What age will you travel to next?

There's a story for every age, from 1 to 100!

 Your mission now is to explore a galaxy far, far away. As you zip through space, you discover a planet never seen before. Color the planet you see out your window.

BRAINSTORM!

What are creative, unforgettable, EXTRAORDINARY names for my planet?

Circle the name you like best!

BRAINSTORM!

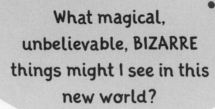

What magical, unbelievable, BIZARRE things might I see in this new world?

Land your spaceship on the new planet. Put on a space suit and go out to explore. ZOTS! It's amazing, like Earth, but in otherworldly ways. Draw a picture.

Next you'll write a story about this planet. Use your brainstorm and picture for ideas of what to say.

Give it all you've got to make it OUT of this WORLD!!!

Put the title of your story in the banner. In the box below, describe what you see from where you stand. How does this place make you feel? Share, in detail, a curious thing you walk toward.

Tell about a life form you hear and see on your trek. What makes you return to your spaceship? Show what you put in your pocket before you board.

 Zap and Gooey are excited to see Sneakers at Becca's party. Pretend they land at YOUR home for a snack along the way. Who else comes over? Draw a picture.

Your family, friends, and neighbors have questions for Zap. What do they want to learn about life on Vox Nova? Write as many questions as you can think of.

THE END

Wait! Turn the page for a BIG surprise . . .

CALLING ALL EARTH KIDS!

Use your imagination to DRAW and WRITE about Zap's or Gooey's body.
Send it in and Zap will email you a note. Get entry info online:
adventureswithzap.com. There's a chance you'll be published on Zap's website!

Play with your imagination and sketch three ideas. Or five. Or more!
Need help? Find pictures of mammals, reptiles, bugs, and birds. Need
extra paper? Go get it!

BRAINSTORM!

What POWER words SHOW what Zap's or Gooey's body looks like and feels like to hug?

Zap has one last thing just for you . . .

Zip-zapper-ZOT! You wrote a LOT!

HERE'S YOUR **Creative Star Award**

STEP 1 Carefully cut the next page from your book. Follow the dotted line that runs from top to bottom.

STEP 2 Cut out your star.

STEP 3 Fill in the blanks on your star.

STEP 4 Ask where you can hang your award. On the wall? The fridge? From your ceiling?

CREATIVE STAR AWARD

This certificate honors

_____
You!

for original, handcrafted art and word play.

Completed this _____ _____, _____.
Month   Date   Year

WHOoo- HOOOoo !!!

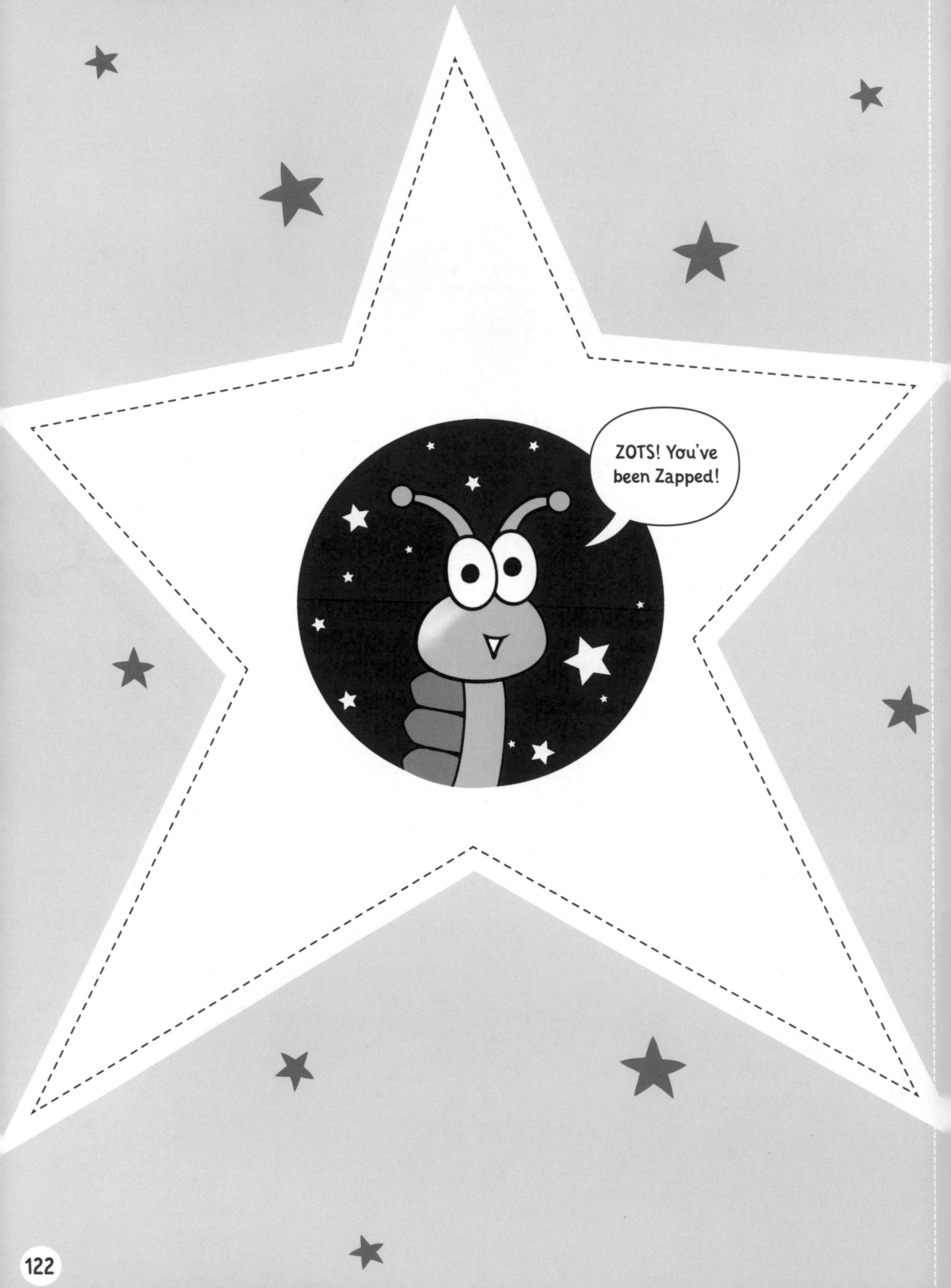
ZOTS! You've been Zapped!

Acknowledgments

The creation of this book was far from a solo journey. There are Earthlings to whom I will forever be grateful for contributing their talents and time.

Every story has a beginning. First on my list of acknowledgments is Jeanne Carriere—a devotee of the late, great Bev Boss—who for five years guided me weekly in her adult education preschool on how to empower children with their voices and create a world of learning through play. Many wonderful K-5 teachers later invited me into their classrooms as a volunteer writing coach, where I learned of the struggles children face and practiced tricks for overcoming them: Mary Spire, Deb Langley, Sara Hapner, Meg Avery, Maryanne Witty, Dean Silvers, Sara Riccabona, Julie Egdahl, Jackie Garcia, James Smith, Jody Lust, Terra Barsanti, Linda Muehlhauser, Joanne Tabasz, and Robin Estrin. I benefited from extra training and extended class projects thanks to writing education advocate Julia Chiapella, Director of the SC-COE's Young Writers Program.

As for my own writing adventure, I'll always be a loyal fan of SCBWI, where I've been (and continue to be) challenged to hone my craft by some the best editors and authors in Kid Lit. I'm also grateful for the fabulous writer friends in my galaxy who critiqued an early draft and provided fountains of support: Carol Foote, Cathe Lieb, Allison Hershey, Jackie Pascoe, Eric Hoffman, Sylvia Patience, Lisa Alexander, and the newest member of our clan, the revered Eve Bunting. Although Eve arrived on the scene too late to preview this book, she fed my spirit with encouragement and bits of wisdom during our many car rides together.

This book would not exist without the clever comic contributions of Allison Hershey, who believed in Zap long before a publisher was part of the picture. I'm awestruck by how she mastered the seemingly impossible task of illustrating Zap and Gooey without revealing their bodies.

Originally thinking I'd self-publish, one question needed answering: would my book inspire children? To find out, I set up a pilot test. The first step was to seek feedback from a group of top-notch teachers whose input helped shape my revision: Dara Thornton, Christy Peterson, Laura Moore, Kendra Carmichael, Karyn Schmidt, Alexandra Muffei, Laura Tobias, Lisa Bagnall, and Samantha Chain. Step two was to recruit a team of Ace Pilot families to play with Zap for a month. These children and caregivers also gifted me with impactful comments, and it was the stories of their experiences that I credit for breathing life into a little blue alien from the planet Vox Nova. I'd like to name them here but made a promise to protect their privacy, though they're the only people on the planet to have earned an Official Zap Pilot license.

More good fortune came my way when angel-in-disguise Brad Wheelwright aligned the stars for a path to professional publication. For those holding this book today, I give a standing ovation to my amazing editor, Anna Bliss, who kept Zap's heart beating throughout the process. Thanks also to Sarah Smith for adding magic touches to every page, and to the other fine folks at The Experiment and Workman who left their thumbprints upon this book.

I'd like to finish this story with a note of eternal gratitude for my family: to my mother for her devotion to education, my father for his patience when nurturing soil and seeds, my husband for his unwavering boosts of morale, and my daughters for their never-ending supply of surprises.

This is my first book. The Earthlings named here are my behind-the-scene heroes and founding members of Zap's tribe. Thanks for helping me get going with another new beginning.

About the Author and Illustrator

About the Author

Diane Landy is a writer of children's fiction and a longtime writing coach in elementary and preschool classrooms. Two of her greatest joys are to inspire new and reluctant writers, and to help young authors of all levels structure their stories and enliven them with details. When not playing with words, she enjoys time with friends and family, creating mosaic art and hiking through the woods. Diane lives in California with her husband, a mischievous elf named Webby, and two empty nests.

About the Illustrator

Allison Hershey's art has appeared in science fiction magazines, anthologies, computer software packaging, and adventure games. As art director and game strategist at the Dreamers Guild she was responsible for visual design and story content. She supervised over twenty artists, creating backgrounds and animation for several computer games, including Inherit the Earth and Faery Tale Adventure: Halls of the Dead. Later, she created the art and dialog for the first five years of a long-running online comic strip: *Inherit the Earth*, based on the original computer game of the same name. She continues to do freelance illustrations for fantasy, science fiction, and children's books.